I0605408

Little People, **BIG DREAMS**™

LEONARDO DA VINCI

Written by
Maria Isabel Sánchez Vegara

Illustrated by
Ana Albero

Frances Lincoln
Children's Books

A long time ago, there was a boy named Leonardo who lived in the town of Vinci, near the city of Florence in Italy. His mind was always full of questions, like how a bat could stay in the air, or what made a star glow.

Raised by his grandfather Antonio and his uncle Francesco, Leonardo didn't go to a regular school but learned freely at home. He loved drawing everything around him to understand it better, and he was really good at it.

Leonardo loved animals and plants as much as he loved sketching them. He drew twisted trees, wildflowers, and the way cats curled up to sleep. At the market, he bought caged birds just to set them free and watch them fly into the sky.

Around the age of twelve, he joined other young artists in a workshop run by the great Andrea del Verrocchio, in Florence. There, Leonardo learned to paint, sculpt, and make bright color powders by crushing plants and stones.

He spent ten years with his teacher, working on many of his artworks. One day, Leonardo painted the face and hair of an angel with such skill that—people said—Verrocchio put down his brush, feeling he couldn't match his pupil's talent.

Yet Leonardo wasn't only drawn to beauty—he was a scientist, too. Understanding how the body worked became a lifelong passion. After leaving Florence, he moved to Milan, where he drew bones and muscles with care.

Leonardo kept notebooks full of detailed drawings and bright ideas about inventions to make people's lives easier. He wrote backwards—perhaps because, as a left-handed writer, it kept the ink from smudging and staining his sleeve.

In Milan, Leonardo worked on a huge religious painting: *The Last Supper*. It showed a long table with thirteen people, all pointing, whispering, or reaching across their plates. It was the most alive painting anyone had ever seen.

Still, his most famous masterpiece wasn't that large mural but a smaller painting called *Mona Lisa*, of a lady with a quiet smile. Leonardo carried it from place to place, adding tiny touches of paint here and there, always smiling back at her.

From dukes to queens, everyone was amazed by Leonardo! He created artwork for walls, chapels, and festivals.

As his fame grew, young artists came to learn from the great master. One of them, Francesco, became as close as family.

One day, Leonardo received a special request: to create something extraordinary for a royal celebration. So, he built a mechanical lion with a heart full of lilies that walked across the room and surprised the King of France.

scuba
suit
parachute
automobile

His Majesty was so impressed by Leonardo's genius that he invited him to live near his palace in France. From his new home, Leonardo continued working, thinking, and dreaming, while his ideas began to travel far beyond time and place . . .

Hundreds of years later, the world is still learning from the questions little Leonardo asked. Through his paintings, notebooks, and inventions, he showed us that trying to understand the world is its own kind of joy.

LEONARDO DA VINCI

(Born 1452 – Died 1519)

c.1470

c.1483 – 1487

Leonardo was born in 1452 near the town of Vinci, Italy. His name "da Vinci" means "from Vinci." Leonardo lived a long time ago so we can't be sure what he looked like. The portraits you see above are thought to be of Leonardo, but we'll never know for certain. At the time Leonardo lived, Europe was going through a period of change called the Renaissance. It was an exciting age of new ideas, scientific discoveries, and great art. When he was around twelve, Leonardo moved to the city of Florence to become an apprentice in the workshop of the artist Andrea del Verrocchio. There, he learned how to make things with his hands: painting, sculpting, and working with metal. Around 1482, he began working as an artist and engineer for the Duke of Milan. Leonardo was interested in so many

c.1512 – 1515

c.1515 – 1518

different things that he didn't always finish everything he started. One of the works he did complete was the *Last Supper*, a huge wall painting for a monastery. Back in Florence a few years later, he began work on another masterpiece: the *Mona Lisa*. In his thirties, he began keeping notebooks filled with sketches, observations, and ideas. There were designs for imaginary cities and extraordinary machines, detailed drawings of the human body, and investigations into the science of flight. Leonardo even drew up plans for a flying machine, hundreds of years before they were invented! He kept writing and sketching in his notebooks his whole life. Leonardo died at sixty-seven years old and spent his last years working for the French king. He is remembered as one of the greatest creators in history.

Want to find out more about **Leonardo da Vinci?**

Have a read of this great book:

The Extraordinary Ideas of Leonardo da Vinci by Alex Woolf

Original idea of the series by Maria Isabel Sánchez Vegara, published by Alba Editorial, S.L.U
"Little People, BIG DREAMS" and "Pequeña & Grande" are trademarks of
Alba Editorial S.L.U. and/or Beautifool Couple S.L.
First Published in the US in 2026 by Frances Lincoln Children's Books, an imprint of The Quarto Group.
Quarto Boston North Shore, 100 Cummings Center, Suite 265D, Beverly, MA 01915, USA
Tel: +1 978-282-9590 **www.Quarto.com**
EEA Representation, WTS Tax d.o.o., Žanova ulica 3, 4000 Kranj, Slovenia. www.wts-tax.si

ISBN 978-1-80570-187-3
Set in Futura BT.

With scientific consultation by Dr. Francesca Borgo, University of St. Andrews

Published by Juliet Matthews · Designed by Sasha Moxon, Izzy Bowman, and Karissa Santos
Edited by Lucy Menzies and Claire Grace · Editorial management by Izzie Hewitt
Production by Robin Boothroyd
Manufactured in Bosnia and Herzegovina
1 3 5 7 9 8 6 4 2

Photographic acknowledgments (pages 28-29, from left to right): 1. David Victorious over Goliath, circa 1470. Found in the Collection of Museo del Bargello, Firenze. (Photo by Fine Art Images/Heritage Images via Getty Images.) 2. Leonardo da Vinci, Portrait of a Musician, painting in oil on panel. 1483 – 1487, incamerastock, ICP, Alamy. 3. Self-Portrait by Leonardo da Vinci. (Inv. 15571, Coll. Dis. It. I/30.) (Photo by DeAgostini/Getty Images.) 4. Portrait of Leonardo da Vinci, circa 1515 – 1518. Found in the Royal Collection, London. (Photo by Fine Art Images/Heritage Images via Getty Images.)

Collect the *Little People,* **BIG DREAMS**™ series:

FRIDA KAHLO
COCO CHANEL
MAYA ANGELOU
AMELIA EARHART
AGATHA CHRISTIE
MARIE CURIE
ROSA PARKS
AUDREY HEPBURN
EMMELINE PANKHURST

ELLA FITZGERALD
ADA LOVELACE
JANE AUSTEN
GEORGIA O'KEEFFE
HARRIET TUBMAN
ANNE FRANK
MOTHER TERESA
JOSEPHINE BAKER
L. M. MONTGOMERY

JANE GOODALL
SIMONE DE BEAUVOIR
MUHAMMAD ALI
STEPHEN HAWKING
MARIA MONTESSORI
VIVIENNE WESTWOOD
MAHATMA GANDHI
DAVID BOWIE
WILMA RUDOLPH

DOLLY PARTON
BRUCE LEE
RUDOLF NUREYEV
ZAHA HADID
MARY SHELLEY
MARTIN LUTHER KING JR.
DAVID ATTENBOROUGH
ASTRID LINDGREN
EVONNE GOOLAGONG

BOB DYLAN
ALAN TURING
BILLIE JEAN KING
GRETA THUNBERG
JESSE OWENS
JEAN-MICHEL BASQUIAT
ARETHA FRANKLIN
CORAZON AQUINO
PELÉ

ERNEST SHACKLETON
STEVE JOBS
AYRTON SENNA
LOUISE BOURGEOIS
ELTON JOHN
JOHN LENNON
PRINCE
CHARLES DARWIN
CAPTAIN TOM MOORE

HANS CHRISTIAN ANDERSEN
STEVIE WONDER
MEGAN RAPINOE
MARY ANNING
MALALA YOUSAFZAI
ANDY WARHOL
RUPAUL
MICHELLE OBAMA
MINDY KALING

IRIS APFEL

ROSALIND FRANKLIN

RUTH BADER GINSBURG

MARILYN MONROE

KAMALA HARRIS

ALBERT EINSTEIN

CHARLES DICKENS

YOKO ONO

MICHAEL JORDAN

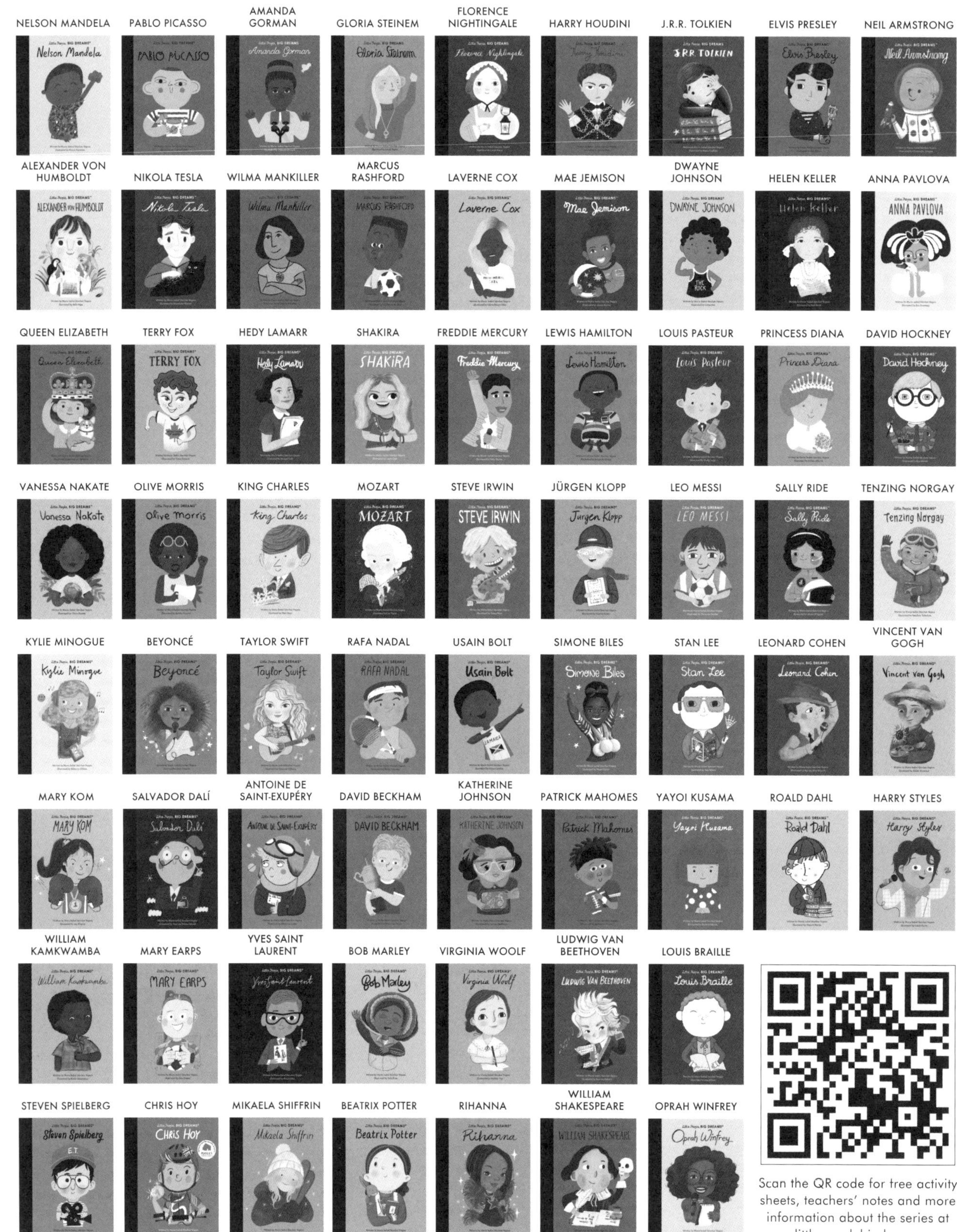
NELSON MANDELA
PABLO PICASSO
AMANDA GORMAN
GLORIA STEINEM
FLORENCE NIGHTINGALE
HARRY HOUDINI
J.R.R. TOLKIEN
ELVIS PRESLEY
NEIL ARMSTRONG
ALEXANDER VON HUMBOLDT
NIKOLA TESLA
WILMA MANKILLER
MARCUS RASHFORD
LAVERNE COX
MAE JEMISON
DWAYNE JOHNSON
HELEN KELLER
ANNA PAVLOVA
QUEEN ELIZABETH
TERRY FOX
HEDY LAMARR
SHAKIRA
FREDDIE MERCURY
LEWIS HAMILTON
LOUIS PASTEUR
PRINCESS DIANA
DAVID HOCKNEY
VANESSA NAKATE
OLIVE MORRIS
KING CHARLES
MOZART
STEVE IRWIN
JÜRGEN KLOPP
LEO MESSI
SALLY RIDE
TENZING NORGAY
KYLIE MINOGUE
BEYONCÉ
TAYLOR SWIFT
RAFA NADAL
USAIN BOLT
SIMONE BILES
STAN LEE
LEONARD COHEN
VINCENT VAN GOGH
MARY KOM
SALVADOR DALÍ
ANTOINE DE SAINT-EXUPÉRY
DAVID BECKHAM
KATHERINE JOHNSON
PATRICK MAHOMES
YAYOI KUSAMA
ROALD DAHL
HARRY STYLES
WILLIAM KAMKWAMBA
MARY EARPS
YVES SAINT LAURENT
BOB MARLEY
VIRGINIA WOOLF
LUDWIG VAN BEETHOVEN
LOUIS BRAILLE
STEVEN SPIELBERG
CHRIS HOY
MIKAELA SHIFFRIN
BEATRIX POTTER
RIHANNA
WILLIAM SHAKESPEARE
OPRAH WINFREY
Scan the QR code for tree activity sheets, teachers' notes and more information about the series at www.littlepeoplebigdreams.com